SONG OF THE TAXIDERMIST

Also by AURIAN HALLER

A Dream of Sulphur

Song of the Taxidermist

AURIAN HALLER

Edited by Anne Compton.
Cover image (top) still from the short film *Mechanism/Organism*, 2006, by Eduardo Menz.
Illustrations from *Practical Taxidermy*, 1992, by John W. Moyer, reprinted courtesy of Krieger Publishing Company.
Cover and page design by Julie Scriver.

Canadian Cataloguing in Publication Date

Haller, Aurian
 Song of the taxidermist / Aurian Haller.

Poems.
ISBN 978-0-86492-649-4

 I. Title.

PS8565.A4547S66 2011   C811'.6   C2010-906092-X

Goose Lane Editions acknowledges the financial support of the Canada Council for the Arts, the Government of Canada through the Book Publishing Industry Development Program (BPIDP), and the New Brunswick Department of Wellness, Culture, and Sport for its publishing activities.

Goose Lane Editions
Suite 330, 500 Beaverbrook Court
Fredericton, New Brunswick
CANADA E3B 5X4
www.gooselane.com

FSC
Mixed Sources
Cert no. SW-COC-000952
© 1996 FSC

pour Caro

Song of the Taxidermist I

Beauty is momentary in the mind —
The fitful tracing of a portal;
But in the flesh it is immortal.

— Wallace Stevens

*

Grin, Niemeyer's Taxidermy, 2005. Polyurethane bear mount

It's best if they bring it in untouched —
most men are butchers with a knife.

All the wild resides in your garage, saved
for their racks, their teeth and fine plumage,

while just across the fields, where new stacks
aim skyward like smoking guns, everything

comes out dog food. Today a bear arrived
in a box: *See what you can do for him*, said

the owner as if to a doctor. The illness,
terminal: death by deflation. The trick is

knowing what he'd been up to the moment
he was surprised by a tingling in his neck.

You can't learn it in books. Even manikin
catalogues are recipes for still lives. Your

grandmother baked by weight, the taste of
rising dough. You know an eighteen-inch

neck just lifting a deer pelt from its box.
See it stretch to meet an itching hind hoof

in a logged clearing, the others sunk in
fireweed. *Shouldn't we all get a second*

chance at beauty? You squat between gallons
of bondo and borax, brushing the doe's

damp throat with your daughter's
brush, or it will dry like that, unnatural.

*

Relay, Niemeyer's Taxidermy, 2005. Zebra legs in taxidermy

These legs would do for table or footstool,
drag boots for women bent on animal

prints. I filled them with what was handy:
firewood from the slumping ravine.

Listen, we are all afraid of abandonment,
but there is nothing to be done.

Think of it as recycling grace. Villagers
thought I was spoiling good meat when I

fibreglassed a sable antelope from the
shoulders up, but they were wasting too:

no one remembers one meal from another.
African sun putrefied the flesh scooped

out, but it mounted fine beside the moose
in my living room. Left to themselves,

legs are inclined to ramble on about hot
savannah, making thunder underfoot,

until they run out of words to describe:
herd, dance, smell of rain before it falls.

It is sight makes us stumble. Around us
are unbroken plains. Around us the crutches

of those who walked away. I set to with
a bucksaw because no one was using them,

and they were beautiful like that, bright
batons in my bag, the long flight home.

＊

Zarafe, Muséum d'Histoire Naturelle de la Rochelle, 1845.
Giraffe in taxidermy

You were famous eighteen years, Egypt's
ambassador to France. Modernism in

walking boots and yellow coat.
Balzac celebrated with a story and

Flaubert held his mother's hand before your
towering metaphor. All of Paris celebrated

polygons: everything "à la giraffe,"
women crouching on carriage floors to

preserve haute coiffure's new heights,
the winter flu your namesake. These days,

you keep company with Empress Josephine's
orangutan, half a dozen shrunken heads,

stuffed with what you dreamed on in winter,
gold fields waving. You used to embody

the Nile; today it's our own past we're
spectating — not so much as a shirr

in the whole animal thanks to arsenic
and good upholstery. Come see

the original tall tale! Seven neck bones
we have in common, insomnia,

an awkward grace. Let's just say
we loved our wonder like teenagers

love vertigo, that's why you're here,
still standing in for something else.

*

7 leagues, Niemeyer's Taxidermy, 2005. Elephant foot in taxidermy

They say in war the most valuable thing
is a pair of good boots — when you fall

they're fair game, back and forth
without taking sides. No one will

bury it, the foot that is. A grave is
for head or heart — house of the eye,

transcriber of dreams, love's red
clutch — may they find rest. Consider

Riopelle's bestiary, all trunk and
ears and darkness below the body.

Our phantoms leave no tracks
by which to follow them home.

Put your ear to the ground, you'll
hear nothing but blood running.

✳

Togo, Iditarod Trail Sled Dog Race Gift Shop / Museum, 1959.
Siberian Husky in taxidermy

Here stands the carrier of the cure for
diphtheria, like last summer's midway prize,

become his own memorial. Two hundred sixty
miles to Bluff in a blizzard — his would be the nose

to follow if the way before you turns to floes, or
a thousand snow geese take to the earth about

your feet. Heroism is measured in ground traversed,
the mercuric winds. Heihachiro Togo sunk the

Russians into the Baltic and became a Shinto kami.
His namesake plunged back into Arctic waters to take

up his broken traces and pull the sled off Norton Sound,
the serum floating like bubbles in a carpenter's level.

To have such singular purpose! Just as surely, the
conditional anterior reeks up from under the fridge

after a freefall off the counter some months ago.
Regret runs in a pack, tongues lolling — who will

finish first? The same who calls up a storm every time
the door opens. What they don't tell is how Togo

escaped after the race to chase reindeer, returned to
the kennel just as satisfied. Does the wishbone

summon the impulse to pull apart, when we carry
all paths within us? Be wary of those that make

all the difference, monuments so sure-footed
in the past, you'd think they were also cast.

*

Novecento, Maurizio Cattelan, 1997. Horse in taxidermy with sling

Instead of boiling down to gelatin,
you swing like a trapeze artist over

the heads of shrieking children. This
is our craft: take a skin and fill it to

the ears with rumination. It will
collect dust somewhere before being

thrown out, soaked up by the garden
like coffee grounds, baiting worms

in the moist earth whose gift is infinite.
Still, not every sparrow's flight is useful:

the unseen flourish to afternoons off
the cliffs where the wind throws you for

a loop. Transfixed, sky and earth
stretch your legs like compass

needles north. See, even the moon is
a hoofprint on the darkening shore.

*

*Natures Mortes: Portrait de Cézanne/Portrait de Renoir/Portrait
de Rembrandt*, Francis Picabia, 1920. Monkey in taxidermy, nails,
board, paint

You're the original still life, nailed
like Curious George to a board.

With this tail, you motion, *I'll
colour your world.* You were

supposed to be caught playing
in the garden, but it's just as well

because you can't hold a pose
around fruit. It's not about you

anyway, you're an exclamation
mark: art is more like the real

world if it's made of the real
world. Trucks shake the street

according to their weight, the
cantaloupe in its bowl collects

flies. You smile at my profile
against the open window. Light

reaches us equally. For the moment,
nothing happens.

*

Monogram, Robert Rauschenberg, 1959. Angora goat in taxidermy,
tire, police barrier, heel of a shoe, tennis ball, oil, metal, wood, fabric,
paper, canvas, and wooden platform mounted on casters

After four years loitering about the studio,
you gave him a canvas to stand on and seeded

it with urban debris. *Be natural,* you said, *think
of the tire around you as a swing, a portal to*

greener pastures. Then you splashed paint
on his face and brushed the treads white, as

if he'd been rolling across the surface of the
moon. We were fed up with illusions and

enigmatic grins. A goat was just what was
needed, something you could grab by the

beard, ride if necessary. When you found
him stuffed on 23rd Street, you were looking

for a new way to paint, to force materials to
speak for themselves. Now, he's an advocate for

the age of juxtaposition. Personally, I prefer
holding the past accountable — your father one

evening with blood on his hands, your mother's
silent apology gives him away. *It's not a dog,*

he says, and you bay at the door closing on
your childhood, its billy ears.

The Swimmers

after paintings (1980-83) by Betty Goodwin

for desire at arm's length
plunges us quickly amid
the sea already blue already drowned

— Nicole Brossard

Dip him in the river who loves water.

— William Blake

Swimmer No. 7, 1982, Oil on vellum

The year I lived in a basement,
the lone window grew all my plants one-sided.
I envied their easy design. Yours is the practice
of suggestion: you assigned your swimmers
the struggle between moving out or being pulled down.
Since painting is an approximation we can't afford
ourselves, should we drift out further
than we thought, *not waving but drowning.*

Meanwhile the earth grew in cross-section
against my windowpane. Below the grass —
roots, dirt, worms who pass it through them
like water.

And reviewers said: what we can't quite make out
completes itself before us, becomes universal;
graphite scratches, oil slips on vellum, draw
out the body's physiognomic clichés
in which we see ourselves reflected.
But twenty-somethings,

even poets, aren't looking for self-recognition.
They worry about the amount of hot water,
because it's an easy grievance. The shuddering pipes are to blame.
I admired Blake for breaking the glass and sounding
the alarm in the first-year textbook etching,
What is Man! Help! Help!

how it cuts to the chase, someone waving
like a dummy in a lifeguard manual:
     this is what to look for, a little red boat
     fitted for rescue.

Swimmers 1980, drypoint in black and blue on laid paper

Your method of rusty cogs and tarpaulins,
naked bodies floating in space — where
every double back is a recovery, burrowing
into the self — assumes so much. Salvage,
for example. My first swim coach said
we swam like minnows in our mothers.

But at the kitchen table I heard
I'd begun to suffocate in the womb, saved
by a broken fetal sac, the uterine air
my first taste of flight. Spiders —

who weave a silk diving bell
and never surface — collect bits of air
like dew off weeds, are their own
submarines.

So I never kept a diary. Already
last summer is like the family cabin —
rice in the salt, storm shutters
drawn. Give me the orange buoy,
something to keep my eye on.
One day, I'll learn the names of tidal grasses,
make a nest of what I know. Rise
and fall.

Swimmer No. 3, 1983, graphite, chalk pastel, oil pastel, and diluted
oil paint on wove paper

If we could switch for a day
I'd paint you leaning against a giant sheet
of Geofilm, a runner
stretching her calves before a race —
no one knows you press the wall
to give in
and have it pull you back.

Buoyancy: the power of fluid
to support a body. It was the material all along
took convincing: let this one be
lucky let this one
pass. All night buoy bells
toll along the St. Lawrence
like floating chapels, while you set out

for rocks. Your erasure
leaves only traces. Wreckage
on the beach. You must be prepared,
you say, to scuttle everything
but take survivors.

You drill holes in them
as if they were shells —
        around your neck this
        new beauty.

I am neither trusting, nor
bold. Bathe me again in light, rub
out the edges. Rough me up.

Study for Berlin Project, 1982, oil on vellum paper

You took pictures from the shallows,
holding the camera as if it could show you
what continuous motion conceals, later
rubbing into the photograph
until only the gesture remained. Your study

stares into the deep, hands
outstretched mid-breaststroke. Exasperation and
obeisance — I'll admit to some of these,
would like to be religious, if only to bow
to something, cast my five limbs
to the earth.

Where I come from the lake has no bottom,
as if the glacier's finger snapped off while digging.
Only by summer's end can you stand
the surface, look down.

Untitled, 1983, black wax crayon and graphite stained with oil on
tracing paper

Refinements of an old skill.
Make the inner outer.
— Phyllis Webb

I take heart in stalactites
dripping into a reversal of themselves,
the way a fallen tree exchanges,
ring by ring, its wooden cells
for lime.

Later, when floods come,
it will stay where it is
and grow weeds on its back.

The sea has emptied into the sky,
and sky-filled canyons.
The body also

learns to wear its label out-
side in, a diver's
imploded suit
                ocean
passing through like a
giant lung.

Untitled, 1982, Oil and graphite on laid paper

The way the river bends makes slow things
sudden, as if we'd turned around to find
everything changed. The cliffs
gone strange in the distilled light. And the gorgons,
leaning since forever,
felled. The boy was
less dramatic. A motionless stage actor,
moving us from within himself,
he floated without muscle or inflation,
his abundance surrounding him
like cork. Had we heard shots to expect
his coming, we would gather
on the sandbar, clutch our sun hats.
But the afternoon stretches like a river,

unbroken over the shallows. This is where
you started before dumping your palate
for tectonic red and black to excavate
the nerves. The surface. It's not a bad thing
to be shallow, where fish swim naked
waiting to be plucked; it's where the present
bruises us. The boy

hears the world through the drum of the river,
his concentration a tightrope walker's
in the half space between his fantasy and
ours, the tug of leaden legs
and the head that doesn't waver;
grinning despite his best efforts
to make us believe.

Moving Towards Fire, 1983, Oil, coloured chalk, and graphite on
woven paper

Apparently you almost drowned as a child.
We all did. It's fear that draws us to trapeze
with a safety net to cradle in, or skydive —
just pull the cord and swell up with air.
I caught my son bobbing in the neighbour's pool,
face down as if looking for something,
his immaculate feet
fluttering. Hummingbirds
at our balcony.

When I was small enough
to fit in a culvert, I crawled
in below the road's centre line,
lay on my back in the dust of August
waiting for cars.
From there everything warned
of a rising flood. From there
dams burst

gasoline. The thought of this
burning in my head, though corrugated metal
is cool on the spine.
Each vertebra finds its place.

Dwelling

L'Habitante

i

Paint these walls. Wake up
       elsewhere
in Peking orange.

Morning in the new room,
hand on the plaster, you are
transported. Spring is this decisive.

You worry our house
as if to convince walls
the roof can support itself.
       They must think up something else to
       stand for.

Curtains like old dresses
 hemmed up (pink knees exposed);
the hat tree's suspect foot; mint
sofa sulking in the hall
like an ex-husband
back for the blender, his mother's china —

              arranging them is
temporary truce.

Only the plants resist being
ordered about.

You wear these spaces
the way a chameleon senses
a subtle shift in the wind —
       and is in turn
       shifted.

Home is a scrubbed shell.
   A soap bowl
gleaned from the Pacific.

Dwelling is an art —
the body   lingering
   also eyes
on something which has,
until now, escaped notice.

How long does each cell last?
The original is a relentless copy,
shedding like goose down
under our bed.

Your bare-knuckle spring
cleaning has nothing to do with germs,
seems pure principle, like clasping hands
to pray, wringing
dry cloth —

repetitive gestures
summoning calm.

iii

An open window
    lights
the moon-dark hall.

Then, we left our beds for
darker pastures; without
blankets to keep us from the
damp and cricket roar,
the mute breathing
of trees,

we did not sleep. Tonight
in this borrowed house
the flood bangs crates and
furniture against the furnace;
basement steps
descending how far?

The rat trap's jaws wait patiently
in the attic, while ants
garrison the kitchen.

There is always a breach. Remember
our rush for duct tape, an airtight
front door? Suspicious powder-
dusted mailboxes — risible flour.

This house is an aquifer.
We try it on; like someone else's clothing,
attractive but alien,
its scent becomes us.

Four Ponies

and now as he lay on his back in the cushioning snow, his knees
gone slack, the horses leaped at and over him, leaped, went up
and over, the shag of winter's bellies went floating up on the
choking snow....

— Robert Kroetsch

i

Tonight horses off their rockers
gallop the toothless earth which,
like an infant, swallows
everything it touches.
We envy their longing

for greener hills.
We are more like the wooden dog
guarding the front door.
Nearly stolen, his stubborn weight
saved him the last leap
over the garden fence.

Now he erodes the front porch
with his chain
while hooves divot up the dark. Tomorrow,

when children find springs and gears
without an excuse to spin
and buck, only the youngest
suspects flight. The rest

feel a brand new pleasure
in absolute blame.

This is not a tower.

Even so, would you tune in?
One station repeating the
Lone Ranger theme like a cricket
indulging its

solitary note. Or else
the *shhh* of hooves
in deep fields. The shallow ocean.

A carousel this far out of town
means the city's rolled onto the Laurentians'
bruised toes. The wind's restless
for something with spring.

For believers, these signs are warnings —
the beginning of the end, the universe
unravelling like a spool of thread.

Outside my window, autumn storms
have not dislodged
the cobweb sail I've been
minding lately.

iii

This garden would gnaw the legs
off a horse!
I feed it eggshells and bones
of small birds, but those

don't satisfy.
All my efforts to curb its dark appetite
with objects of beauty
fall prey.

We choose our ornaments
to uncover which corner of our
dim kingdom needs light.

iv

K&K Pet Foods, jazzed up
by horses ready to prance on the spot,
is selling recycled hooves
delicious in bags and tins.

The quarter drops
and a worn saddle swings
its stirrups with precise enthusiasm.

Who are the cannibals
when there aren't enough
holes in the earth for our
belongings, or angels to guard
the exits from
new towers?

So why not   41
a horse instead of a cross?
God knows there are enough loads
left to carry.

Salvage

Reach under the bumper,
a hook for just such
        slips. It's all planned
by engineers, probability factors.
Early snow soft as fur.

But the body's made
seamless
as if it were an insult to assume
assistance will be needed.

Remember the moose
too stubborn for ropes?

She'll poison the hole she drank from,
said the farmer, *it's either her*
or the cows.

Impressed with such
moral precision, we watched
men in overalls approach with guns;
her eyes already leaving a shadow
in the water hole for the approaching tractor,
levered bucket, the unrelinquishing earth.

It's not for beauty we adorn
our ears and nose, stubborn
lower lip, lunar navel but
purchase, the chance to be led
forward from the mud's cold suck

into the shivering sun.

Decoy

My grandmother picked easily
from years of bending to small things;

the berries tattooing her hands in the ditch
where Oregon grape grows best.

She didn't like to be watched,
but forgot to notice. How many
more harvests.

The Tutchone have spirit houses for those
whose bodies go missing: carried off

by river, float plane, or crow, the spirit
is lured back like a duck to its

wooden twin in the reeds.
What are poems if not houses? Here

is a door I have hinged and set ajar.
Can we return again once we've
tasted flight?

The berries were steamed, the juice
boiled with sugar. There are still jars enough
for another winter.

Faith is the practice of ingestion, wings
filled with the stuff they beat against.

Plantings

1.

In these parts, ground must be broken
before frost: shovelhead to bedrock
where tired pines relinquish their roots to
dance with the wind. We planted

an empty bucket for your winter plot
to let the earth get used to the feeling of space.
    Just yesterday Ocean Spray bloomed
    here, white surf in the brush.

Now is no surplus. The light,
harsh with nothing to rest on.

Bears wait for darkness: our spirit selves
done with the season.

2.

Weeks on we climb the hill, processional
in a narrow snow track, use flashlights
and tall boots as if traversing a great distance.
Someone pulling a sled with loose dirt and

a hammer to crack the urn.
If we look up in darkness, it is not to see
but to feel snow fall. We resist
the eye's monopoly on memory,
make ghosts
    just breathing.

Belongings

1. Letter Opener

could not cut the firmest tomato,
must feel good
to hold,
ceremonial.
You're more likely to bleed
from paper or the message it carries.
Handwritten mail sits
at the bottom where you'll take
greater care in teasing out its contents.
A knife has a crooked grin, while the opener,
a sheep
seeking gentle passage,
follows the fold.

2. Bird

whose wooden back
eased the palm of your hand, as if
resting there
could teach a human to roost.

There is no logic to what remains,
just that it sustained the years,
took them underwing.

3. Salt Cellar

with its spoon by the stove
has fooled guests too young to know
the rank of salt
and spoiled their coffee.
    Judas was careless at the table
    and spilled his own end.
Just a dash draws out shy flavours,
or water from yellow straightnecks and
purple eggplants. We travelled from
Sunday dinners with
its blessing on our tongues
accipe sal sapientiæ
may wisdom flavour all your days.

47

4. Glove

outside my window a rat grown
flatter and wider all week
under traffic — to the point where it's
encompassing more of the road,

loses all semblance of rat.
He could be a glove missing
its match. Across the city

a hand clenches
like a wet animal
seeking cover.

My son's dance down the hall
is translucent, the bath
still glowing in him, while

my grandmother,
whose skin is like butter,
wears rubber to handle dishes.
All the breakable things
which cannot be grasped.

Tales of Unrest

1.

There are walls in this house
entirely committed to the contours
of your face: all its moods and
background lands.

The winter we were house-sitting,
even the pebble
next to the owner's bathtub
wore the miniature likeness of a guru.

    I thought how obsessive and complete
    this need to bathe in the constant
    presence of love.

While you sleep, walls breathe
like folded wings. An empty hallway
idles, new chimes on the deck hum

    tunelessly,
while I make coffee
and clean.

2.

If your appetite were life-size,
no bridge could bear its stamping
feet. As it is, the tenants cringe
the moment its toes touch
the morning floor.

Nothing should be bland; curries
and garlic are soap bubbles to catch the senses
up through the bannister's iron rails.
The rest collects around your chair
like spent confetti.

What food would I be?
Yams, sweet without seasoning
and good for the soul.

3.

When you look up from your basket,
we're recognized, though you're probably
drawing a blank. You're the only person we can
peer into, like an empty drawer. Imagine
hearing a river beyond the alders
and finding a pool's
shallow stones.

4.

Red shoes drying on the doorstep
tell all there is to know about dew.

We no longer mark time as
ebb and flow, but a body shifting,
a growing weight;
the way an old man's satchel
on a long journey

begins in his arms,
then on his back, then drags behind
catching on rocks and other
points of interest.

5.

There are telltale signs —
Conrad's *Tales of Unrest* crumpled
in the bamboo thicket of your room,
blue mouthfuls of tubercular crayons — the rest
slip out of mind without fanfare.

Who can mark the depths your body
plumbs each night while I lie too lightly
in another room? We can only bottle the

conspicuous: an old woman's scent
outlives its wearer in
garage-sale suitcases.

You are the smell of water that
holds the trace of even
its largest container, just.

6.

You are already up to your elbows
in the past, albums propped open
like travel maps on the floor:

here are mountains, kitchens and
rivers to the sea, familiar because
visited yesterday, because you are
in them, waving.

This is the way we remember. Not
the burst of gunpowder, tomatoes,
or sex, but glaciers retracing
a trail gone cold. When it happens,
it's no accident.

Five Drownings

We're called to life
by water, some of us. Unable to conform within.

— Anne Compton

1. hesitation

When the land they spoke of flooded,
it was the end of words.

The beauty of water is its
ambivalence — after quenching
taproots,
        it's off to gnaw
sandstone petroglyphs
until they slough into the sea.

My wife was taken by the river,
as if violence were an act
committed by the world
while he watched from a distance,

the current swayed by guilt.

But she's become
a sunken valley
used to a watery sky,
artificial banks, severed
roads.

September salmon arrive to find
the river large as an inland sea,
swim up the tarmac's yellow line
like limber traffic,
passing through.

2. ballast

Be water,
find a lower place, go there.
— Roo Borson

He wants the girl to feel depth
as direction.

It's hard to gauge the flow
of a tidal river without
putting your hand in.
As the skin dries, it quickly
forgets.

See here, the man exposes
piano wire like a mole's
tendons, *this is how it works.*
The thicker the strand, the deeper
its note.

He puts lead shot in the girl's left
shoe. And the ball of her foot
swings heavy all afternoon.

Years later she'll recall
a glass of water, its slow
spill over hardwood floor;
dog hair and grass,
the reprimand.

There are other ways
to remember.

The body finds its own
slow glissando to the lowest point,
where it hovers,
disappears.

3. fatigue

No one saw the gymnast's calculated
leap into the canyon, bike tires
drifting from her like
spinning planets —

a vanishing trick
into erupting foam,
skill of somersaults
over rapids, rocks.
Blue flash of nerve out
the culvert's smoking barrel,

past anglers with eyes
in their hands, the shallow
sandbars.

Left with a muddy equation
(velocity times angle of descent),
police don't know where to look.
Search dogs? Who's surprised
they bark at nothing, the lake
too limpid now for riddles.

Every pool has a still point,
where water congeals.
This is where she's anchored,

night snorkeller
among deadwood, fish
too tired to swim.

4. surrender

Dying is stepping out of a lake
into warm rain, his father said,
and slipped away like snowpack in a heat wave —
           you don't notice until you
             look up.

To keep afloat he fills sandbags,
losing his yard to the lake
in fathoms — the height of
a man wading,

           the sump pump
           a heart
           beating
           in the basement.

How high will it go? He calls
old friends and watches mountains
grow green, fish swim beneath
his tomato pots.

Nothing to be done but wait it out —
like the herons captaining the patio furniture,
the barbecue's black reef, bedsheets
sailing over the yard.

There are many forms of grief.

The basement doors
wash open,
close like twin rudders.

5. mercy

The best way to snuff a litter
is in a pot of boiling water.

Ready? he asks,
as though I could
brace for it, a muscle
flexing, and he were a magician;

legs (not mine) leaping
at the far end of a sawn box.

I'm six — a year for each kitten
in the shoebox I'm holding.
Hot water, he says,
saves the trouble of
pushing them under.

He spoons them one by one
like blind dumplings
into soup,

the kitchen bathed
in the warm cupboard
smell of being born.

Speechless

It is an unfortunate fact that speech does not fossilize...

— W. Tecumseh Fitch

*

Now there's less to rattle around,
said the doctor, and removed his gloves.

I looked in beyond my son's enamel
pebbles, raspberry tongue, soft palate's

basaltic ridges — the familiar characters.
The offending flaps were gone, too small to be

missed, but my boy sounded like somebody
else's. A month later, he'd retuned himself:

the voice banging around down there, come
up with a hammer, all spark and flourish.

*

We're born to breathe and suckle at the
same time — tongue-tied until the voice box

drops down the throat like a parachuter
suspended from silk ligaments and tree limbs.

The body is an instrument of precision:
Turkana Boy's rib cage (ca 1.5 million)

was not sufficiently tuned for speech.
All this to show what took us ages has a

reasonable explanation. But there's nothing
for the record but the hyoid bone, trampled

parade baton. Certainly not Tut's trumpets
heralding the birth of jazz. Origin is no

port of departure. An intake of breath
marks the phrasing. Consider the whisper:

fluent in every phoneme, though its vowels
wheeze like organ bellows and the reeds,

unbended. Someone pulls the stops and
the empty place is filled. The head is not a

crown, but a chamber resonating the note,
its beautiful escapes.

*

Any adaptations produced by evolution are useful only in
the present, not in some vaguely defined future.
— Steve Olson

There's a family in London no one can talk to.
It seems some metabolic pathways

are in error. And no syntax in these homes.
Elbows on the table, leftover gerunds, the usual

epithets. At least this time, you can
blame the parents. Still, we pass ourselves

down with the best of intentions.
There is something irrefutable

and therefore religious about this. Who's
going to argue with the unseen, single

explanation? A coiled worm, really, with
a vigorous promoter has been keeping us

up to date. Everyone, that is, but the above.
Just to remind us one step sideways stops the

poem in its tracks. Those whales that shed
their legs to return to the depths of the sea.

*

Most things can be exposed with a sharp
object — ripe pomegranate or a Neanderthal's

brain not capable of a full range of vowels,
the seedy purpose lodged in the prefrontal cortex.

There is a long explanation for desire: axons
reaching out like fingers in a bucket chain.

How were we to know who'd get the message
and start brimming? One day we woke from a

dream so real our head bones swelled for
the telling and we painted epics in the air

with elegant fingers, thespian brows, the
whites of our eyes. Our mouths, just rude

accompaniment: stutter and haw like ducks'
feet beating the water, while wings told the

story of flight. The knowing glance was
invented so we could share the moment

without getting in its way. The body lifts
and catches the wind, sails off speechless.

*

We began by aping the loon at sundown,
goose chatter among the decoys, spray

of slate along the narrow trail. They gave
voice to loneliness, cheery ignorance, our

rocky grip on the world. The real virtuosos
are songbirds outlasting the morning because

females fall for big repertoires, the strutting
oratorio's meaningless complexity. My

daughter throws her voice like champagne
flutes against the wall without a thought

to bare knees. No other primate revels in such
waste. There are chores to be done and children

to feed. A waxing moon is nothing to howl
about. Where did the Fall go? We tasted

cardamom in the wind down the mountain
and forgot the hunt, returned to the fire empty-

handed, our mouths full of pods. When you
can husk with your teeth, you develop a

taste for consonants — the space between
easy as breathing out. You start singing

in the shower, the water pours down.
You could drain a lake with this song.

69

Song of the Taxidermist II

C

*

L'Homme à la mandibule, 1776-1781. Honoré Fragonard. Skinned
cadaver with donkey jawbone

*The painter who has acquired a knowledge of the nature of the
sinews, muscles and tendons will know exactly in the movement of
any limb how many and which of the sinews are the cause of it....*
                                              — Leonardo da Vinci

i

Draw the skin like a curtain spotlighting the
body's constant grin. Map its veins with wax

and alloys, dress it in a lacquer coat to make a
human window. What do you see? The seat

of reason is the mass of a cabbage; as of birth the
fist grows in tandem with the heart until it shakes

in traffic jams at cars cutting in, or sits in the lap like
a dying bird, sunspotted. This is cold science and

students will benefit from such precision. Anatomy
is the sum of its parts: the room is white, the coats

and tiles also so that shadows are accounted for.
You are the pedant in the family. Only brother to

the famous painter, but you share his illusions.
Anyone can see there are other possibilities

for each natural occurrence. You take your
scalpel and consider where to begin.

73

L'homme 1149 is of average height with good
musculature, a manual labourer, used to gripping

tools and taking orders. You open him like a welder
the hull of a ship, or something burrowed out —

bees in the carcass of a lion; jugulars, flapping
bootlaces; trapezius and deltoid, uprooted

saplings. Ears and lips shrivel into a snarl, the sunken
nose, jutting penis; eleven operations by candlelight

to give the body back its natural poise because we're
not made of clay with its riverbank-way of giving

in when pressed. Flesh remembers how it pulled
the bones out of bed in the morning, punched a kid

on the bridge after the heat wave, rain and blood
sweet relief — even here on a table in this cold room.

iii

Give a man a sceptre to rouse a king, a scroll
to make a scholar. You grant him the jawbone

of an ass and summon up the original hulk. Behold
the berserker, a handy fellow in a tight spot,

swinging his bone around like a scyther in a field,
not what St. Francis had in mind when he dubbed

his body "brother donkey," a dead weight even his
god couldn't shed fast enough. The nature of

sinews is light: in one window, out another. What
we call nightmare is testament to your *creature of a*

different kingdom, dancing for you exotic *sarabandes;*
even the soul stands lead-footed before it.

75

Notes

"Grin" includes a quotation from the author's interview with Haze Niemeyer at Niemeyer's Taxidermy.

"Togo" refers to the overlooked hero of the successful transport of diphtheria serum by dogsled relay from Anchorage to Nome, Alaska in 1925. Since Balto finished the relay, Togo missed his chance to become a media celebrity, immortalized in bronze in Central Park and on the silver screen.

"Swimmer No. 7" includes a quotation by Betty Goodwin in an interview with Robert Enright. The second quotation in "Swimmer No. 7" is by the poet Florence Margaret, better known as Stevie Smith. The poem is entitled, "Not Waving But Drowning."

The photos in "Four Ponies" were taken by the author in Athens, Georgia; Saint-Eustache, Quebec; and Vancouver, British Columbia.

"Decoy," "Plantings," and "Belongings" are all written in memory of my grandmother Baba.

The title "Tales of Unrest" is taken from Joseph Conrad's book of short stories by the same name.

The poem "Speechless" is a poetic argument for the origin of language, something that has been hotly debated in and between the fields of anthropology, paleontology, primatology, speech physiology, forensic anthropology, archaeology, evolutionary linguistics, neuroscience, biology, and genetics.

The italics in part three of "Song of the Taxidermist II" are the translated words of Marcel Proust, who was, at the time he wrote them, lamenting his mother's failing health.

References

Blake, William. *The Complete Poetry and Prose of William Blake*. ed. David V. Erdman. New York: Doubleday, 1988, 35.

Borson, Roo. *Water Memory*. Toronto: McClelland and Stewart, 1996, 39.

Brossard, Nicole. *Museum of Bone and Water*. trans. Robert Majzels and Erin Mouré. Toronto: House of Anansi Press, 1999, 28.

Compton, Anne. *Processional*. Markham: Fitzhenry and Whiteside, 2005. 85.

Fitch, W.T. "The evolution of speech: A comparative review." *Trends in Cognitive Sciences* 4.7 (2000): 262.

Kroetsch, Robert. *The Studhorse Man*. Toronto: Random House, 1970, 31.

Olson, Steve. *Mapping Human History: Discovering the Past Through Our Genes*. New York: Houghton Mifflin Books, 2000, 87-88.

Stevens, Wallace. *Harmonium*. New York: Alfred A. Knopf, 1923, 34.

Wallace, Robert, Ed. *The World of Leonardo 1452-1519*. New York: Time-Life Books, 1966, 131.

Webb, Phyllis. *The Vision Tree: Selected Poems*. Vancouver, Talon Books, 1982, 127.

Acknowledgements

Versions of some of these poems have appeared in *The Malahat Review, The Antigonish Review, Queen's Quarterly,* and *Arc.* My thanks to the editors of each. The title poem won the 2007 *Malahat Review* Long Poem Prize as well as the gold medal in the 2007 National Magazine Awards. It also appeared in *The Best of Canadian Poetry in English,* published by Tightrope Books. A selection from "Belongings" won third prize in the *2007 Arc* Poem of the Year Prize. "The Swimmers" was shortlisted in the 2008 CBC Awards for Poetry.

My thanks to Gary Geddes, Jennica Harper, and Ian Rae for their comments on particular poems. Gratefulness to Laisha Rosnau for swapping manuscripts one winter. To Julie Scriver for putting pictures to these words. To my editor Anne Compton, for her promised frankness and attentive ear, the sly turn that makes all the difference. To Caroline and my family, for sharing with me all the strange lands and spaces from which these poems were born.

AURIAN HALLER is an award-winning poet and singer-songwriter.
He is the lead singer of the aurian haller band, whose unique blend
of folk, rock, and jazz is supported by Haller's haunting lyrics. Haller's
poetry has appeared in *Arc, Descant, The Antigonish Review,* and in
his acclaimed collection *A Dream of Sulphur.* He has won numerous
national awards, including a National Magazine Award for poetry
and the *Malahat Review* Long Poem Prize. Haller grew up in the
foothills of the Rockies and now lives in Quebec City.